Cape

Inua Ellams

T0316279

methuen | drama

LONDON • NEW YORK • OXFORD • NEW DELHI • SYDNEY

METHUEN DRAMA
Bloomsbury Publishing Plc
50 Bedford Square, London, WC1B 3DP, UK
1385 Broadway, New York, NY 10018, USA

BLOOMSBURY, METHUEN DRAMA and the Methuen Drama logo are
trademarks of Bloomsbury Publishing Plc

First published in Great Britain by Oberon Books 2013

This edition published 2020

A catalogue record for this book is available from the British Library.

A catalog record for this book is available from the Library of Congress.

ISBN: PB: 978-1-3502-0465-2
ePDF: 978-1-3502-0466-9
eBook: 978-1-3502-0467-6

Series: Plays for Young People

Typeset by Mark Heslington Ltd, Scarborough, North Yorkshire

To find out more about our authors and books visit
www.bloomsbury.com and sign up for our newsletters.

Introduction

Synergy Theatre Project aims to aid the rehabilitation and resettlement of prisoners and ex-prisoners and prevent young people from entering the criminal justice system through access to high quality theatre. Our young peoples' programme aims to engage those young people most at risk of or already involved with offending to inspire change by capturing the imagination and challenging attitudes, motivations and behaviours.

Synergy Theatre Project and the Unicorn Theatre co-commissioned and co-produced *Cape* in 2013, touring the play to secondary schools across London before a run at the Unicorn Theatre. Alongside the tour Synergy produced an education pack for teachers. Below are some extracts from this pack, detailing a theme from the text.

The sections contain a warm-up exercise, which practically helps introduce the theme, a drama or writing exercise to help explore the text further and some questions for provoking further discussion.

Theme One: Boundaries

People are responsible for their own behaviour, their physical and emotional well-being. As citizens and members of the community people look out for each other, look after each other and protect and defend each other but ultimately people can only be responsible for their own behaviour and boundaries. In *Cape*, every single character goes beyond personal boundary and 'crosses a line' which has consequences for the other characters.

Warm-up Exercise: Bomb and Shield

Good for: Creating energy, physical warm up

Useful outcomes: Becoming more aware of everyone in the room and of your own boundaries.

Props: None

Basic rules: Everyone finds a space in the room and looks around. Each person must decide on a person who becomes their 'bomb'. They then must choose another person is their 'shield'. They must try and stay as far as possible away from their bomb and try to keep the shield between them and the bomb. Nobody should touch anyone else. After a while shout freeze and the group must stay still. People can try and guess who was someone's bomb/shield. Find out who has succeeded and who hasn't.

Advanced variation: Play in pairs. When you shout freeze, discuss the shapes created in the space and what kind of scene it could be.

Questions to ask at the end relating to themes in the play:

Did you manage to keep the boundary of the Shield being between you and the Bomb?

As people had conflicting movements how did that affect your ability to not touch anyone else and keep that physical boundary?

Discuss that feeling of people being unpredictable and chaotic with their behaviour as they tried to stick to their objective. How does this relate to the characters in the play and their objectives?

Drama Exercise

In groups choose one of the characters from the play and discuss where they think they 'cross a line'.

Create a physical tableau to show this moment in detail.

Discuss what each character in this image is thinking about or feeling and why they make that decision.

Devise/write an imaginary speech bubble of what each character in the image is thinking.

Now create what happens just before to instigate them crossing the line:

This could also be a still image;

Or this could be dialogue for a scene that we never see in the actual play.

It could be a confession/monologue to the audience.

Create an alternative ending – what might happen if those lines hadn't been crossed:

This could be a still image;

A still image with words;

Or a short, devised scene

Discussion Questions

At what point did each of the characters 'cross the line'? Were there definitive actions of was there a gradual slip? Do you all agree where these are?

How far would you go to protect/defend someone else?

Is it ever right to use force against another person? When?

What are your own personal boundaries?

Theme Two: Use of Self-Defence

In *Cape* the characters of Bruce, Uhuru, Ama and Smithy all use self-defence. There is a growing sense of fear in the community about crime and the attacker who hasn't been caught. Uhuru trains members of the community to defend themselves from attack using martial arts. Bruce carries a screwdriver and tries to persuade Ama to carry a homemade taser in case she is attacked again. Smithy has been trained by the police force to protect the community and himself. He carries a baton.

Gov.uk states that a person may use reasonable force in defence of themselves or another person.

Opinions differ on what constitutes reasonable force. The following games and exercises explore this theme and the law.

Warm-up Exercise: Coin Tag

Good for: Physically getting warm, breaking barriers in the group, playing a very clear objective, concentration and focus.

Useful outcomes: Exploring how fear can affect a group's behaviour. Exploring how members of a group respond to 'attack' and how they might defend one another.

Props:

Enough coins (1ps and 2ps) for everyone in the group to have two, although you can play with one.

Music (this is not essential but using music to underscore can help the energy in the room)

Basic rules: Everyone finds a space in the room. Everyone balances a coin on the back of their non-dominant hand. They can hold another spare coin in the same hand. When the music starts, they must try and steal as many coins from other people as possible without having theirs stolen. Once their coins have been stolen they are out. It is good to set a time limit on this. The winner is the person with the most coins.

Advanced variations:

Play in teams. The teams must try and keep each other in the game as long as possible. They can share their spare coins out to members of their team to keep them in. The winner is the team with the most coins.

Play in different sized teams. This way you can explore the imbalance of power. This raises the stakes and introduces a much higher level of fear. You can also give teams unequal powers. One group may all start with two coins while another with only one coin. This way you can explore the notion of power and privilege for certain groups and how this affects their confidence and ability to win.

Questions to ask at the end relating to themes in the play:

In *Cape* the community feels increasingly unsafe as eight attacks take place and no one is caught. They all find different ways to cope with uncertainty and fear. It also affects the way they look out for each other. In Coin Tag you are always looking over your shoulder waiting for someone to try and steal your coin.

What kinds of emotions did this game evoke for you? Suspicion? Fear? Aggression? Focus?

What did you observe about other people? In the play all the characters deal with fear and helplessness differently. How did you respond?

What was it like playing on your own? In the play Smithy is often separate from the community. What is this experience like? Did anyone in the game begin to look out for anyone else instinctively? If so, why?

What was it like playing in a pair? Explore the notion of a relationship, of someone looking out for you or being let down by them. In the play Smithy and Uhuru are looking out for Bruce, Bruce is looking out for Ama. The characters have a sense of responsibility and care for each other. How did that affect the way you played? Which character are you most like?

What was it like playing in a team? What does it feel like to be part of a strong community? How well did your team work together? If the teams were unequal in size and ability how did that affect morale and your strategy/confidence? How might this relate to the notion of community in the play? Did it make you angrier and more determined or less committed to the objectives of the game? What natural leaders (like Uhuru) emerged?

Writing Exercise: If I Could Go Back

Each person should choose one of the characters from the play.

They should find a space in the room and spend a couple of minutes thinking through that person's story and the attack. Use the following questions to prompt their imagination.

What happened?

What did you think was happening?

What time was it?

Did you know that place well?

Why were you there?

What did you want?

What were you feeling?

Who else was there?

What were they talking about?

How did you feel about that?

What did you feel just before it happened?

How did you feel after?

What happened afterwards?

At the top of the page they should write 'If I could go back...' and they must then write continuously for a designated period. Spelling, punctuation and grammar are irrelevant. The pen should not leave the page. It may be helpful to play some music to underscore this exercise. The questions should help get into the characters head so they can write. Length is not important.

The group should work in pairs to put together a one-minute performance of their two monologues. They may wish to do their own, choose an extract, swap them and perform someone else's or splice them together.

Discussion Questions

What do you think about self-defence after watching this play? Has your opinion changed at all? What is reasonable force?

Which characters were 'rational' when they used self-defence and who was responding 'emotionally'? Were they aware of that?

What is 'reasonable' when emotions are high?

What else – besides reason – influences our responses?

What are some of the emotions that influenced the characters in the play? (Fear, anger, revenge, etc.)

Are there things they could have done that would have prepared them better?

If you could advise the characters personally what would you say?

How might this apply to your own life?

Theme Three: Different Perspectives on Crime in the Community

The characters in *Cape* witness, or are part of, many of the same events. However, they all perceive what exactly happened and the intentions of other characters very differently. There are multiple perspectives that help us find out what happened and why characters behaved and responded the way they did.

Warm-up Exercise: Une, Deux, Trois, Soleil

Good For: Focus, teamwork, precise movement, bluffing, exploring power dynamics.

Useful Outcomes: This game explores how individuals respond to authority, how they work together to achieve something, and what happens when one person is given power that others don't have.

Props: A small object.

Basic rules:

A person is designated as 'The Official' and stands at one end of the space. The rest of the group form 'The Collective' at the other end of the space.

The Official places an object by her feet and faces away from the The Collective.

Their objective is to sneak up on her and steal the object and smuggle it back to their corner without being caught.

When her back is turned they creep towards her. She warns them by saying 'Une Deux Trois Soleil' before she then turns to face them. If she catches an individual moving, she uses her power to punish them by sending them back to their base. She can be as ruthless as she likes looking for movement.

Once the group have stolen her object they must hide it from her and bluff who has it while they attempt to get it back to their corner.

Once stolen, each time she turns, rather than send someone moving back she is allowed to make a guess as to who has the object. This continues until either The Collective win by successfully getting the object back without being caught or The Official catches a culprit red handed who becomes the next 'Official'.

Advanced variation:

The Collective must attempt to complete the task but attached to each other. If they move, they must disentangle themselves from the group without moving someone else or that person will also be punished. This time instead of sending them back The Official makes them do five press-ups/sit-ups.

Questions to ask at the end relating to themes in the play:

What does it feel like to be The Official and separate from The Collective? How did you use your power? How harsh were you? What seemed fair to you? Was anything frustrating?

What does it feel like to be part of The Collective? What were the frustrations? What was good? Did you come together as a united community with a common purpose or were there different agendas? What does it feel like when everyone is working together against The Official? What happens when members of the gang don't play with as much effort? Does anyone do anything unusual and if so why? How does loyalty and relationship come in to play here?

What was The Collective's relationship with power like? How did you feel towards The Official's authority?

What strategies did The Collective have to use to succeed?

Writing Exercise: Different Versions of the Same Event

In pairs ask them to either:

Choose an anecdote which contains conflict from their own life

Choose a story from a newspaper (it is better to use an example from your own life but if this is going to be problematic use a newspaper story)

Tell the story. If the story is theirs, ask them to refer to themselves as 'he/she' (in the third person) to allow some distance from it. Are they able to tell it in a way that their partner doesn't know which person is them?

Then choose two people who were there. Think about how they would tell the story to make themselves the centre of it. Discuss what both people wanted or might have wanted. Discuss whether they got what they wanted. How did they feel before and after this moment? Who had the most power?

Think about the following things: where it took place, what happened, who was there, what could they see/touch/smell/taste/hear, what tiny details stick out. Can they describe the place? If they don't know – invent details.

Each partner sits and writes a version of the story from a specific character's point of view. If the story belongs to one of the partners take the other person's side. They can decide whether they are talking directly to the audience, to themselves or to someone else. The monologues above are all directed at those in authority over the character.

Read aloud. What similarities and differences are there? Are there justifications and explanations?

Explore staging a one-minute version of these.

Discussion Questions

What do each of the characters feel about their community? How does this differ?

How do the characters respond to authority/power?

How does that affect what happens in the play?

Who has authority in your community?

How do you respond to authority figures?

How does it help to imagine the same story from a different perspective?

Cape

Characters

Tanya
Bruce
Smithy
Uhuru
Ama

Act One

Tanya   ACTION! A simple bus stop on a side street at night, old lottery tickets litter the ground like large confetti.

Bruce   The more time you waste, the more time he's got to get away. Just tell me what I need / to know to find

Tanya   I'm setting the scene, the best writers do that.

Bruce   Get to the point. WHO DID IT?!

Tanya   That's not the point!

Bruce   God! You're so . . . COME ON, TANYA!

Tanya   I'm not telling you like that.

Bruce   And what's with the whole action and cut thing?

Tanya   Coz it's like a film . . . what happened. It's not clear like . . . and whatisname should direct it . . . who made *Batman*?

Bruce   Christopher Nolan.

Tanya   Yeah . . . crazy timelines, mad stunts, body doubles and stuff.

Bruce   You gonna sell the story to Christopher Nolan?

Tanya   Why not? It's a good one.

Bruce (*laughs*)   Nutter.

Tanya   Isn't it?

Bruce   You're mad, Tanya.

Tanya   Admit it!

Bruce   Just tell me who so I can . . . please, Tanya?

Tanya   Naa, Bruce, that won't help, you gotta listen, just trust me.

Bruce   Tanya, if you don't / tell me

Tanya   What? . . . You're not sure who it is, so you can't do anything. You're stuck here, might as well listen.

Bruce   I . . . fine . . . whatever.

Tanya   Yesss . . . Okay, I'll start from the top. A simple bus stop on a side street at night, old lottery tickets litter the ground like large confetti. On the red plastic bench, someone's written 'eff the police' with a thick black marker, there's a bin spilling parking tickets out across the street and the one fluorescent light is blinking. There's a mother / Uhuru Moses

Bruce   *Our* mother.

Tanya   Fine then, Mum, Uhuru Moses

Bruce   Yep.

Tanya   and a policeman.

Bruce   Constable Smith.

Tanya   Yeah, but they don't know him yet.

Bruce   They don't?

Tanya   Don't think so.

Bruce   Okay . . . alright. Mum, PC Smith and Uhuru Moses. Carry on.

Tanya   Gotta do it properly . . . Scene, characters aaaaaaannnnd action!

Smithy *is aggressive, shouting almost,* **Uhuru** *speaks calmly,* **Ama** *is scared.*

Smithy   We, officers, who police these streets, take our jobs very seriously / we dedicate

Uhuru   Ama, stand back from this lunatic.

Smithy   We execute the law to the letter, with transparency.

Uhuru   How many black men have died in your custody? How many officers have been charged? Where is the transparency?

Smithy   The entire police force cannot be condemned for the actions of a few.

Uhuru   Stop and search policy? You treat my entire community as criminals because of the actions of a few.

Ama   Gentlemen, calm down.

Smithy   That policy is a preventative measure.

Ama   Uhuru, step back from the policeman.

Uhuru   You want to prevent crime? First, stop supporting a system that directly profits from and necessitates crime; politicians who are criminals, companies breaking tax laws.

Smithy   Those are separate issues.

Uhuru   Allow me to link them for you. Every time / a young person is

A figure dressed in black jumps from the shadows and attacks **Ama**. **Smithy**, *on hearing her scream, pulls out a baton and smacks the figure till the figure falls and keeps swinging, frustration pouring out onto the figure.*

Smithy   Arghh stop! Stop it! Stop that! That's not what happened and you know it. Think we're heartless, stone cold bastards, love violence, think we've no conscience? Love our batons? Breaking knuckles? Cracking heads? Blood on pavements, think we're like this? I believe in justice; it's a honourable thing, this badge means we uphold the law, protect what we love, that's our task, police the country, protect its bridges, alleys, tunnels, streets, even the bus stops. Some nights in the squad car, when everything is still, there's a quietude, a tranquility settles on the city. A sleeping urban forest, litter like fallen leaves, puddles are small rivers, street lights are trees, and we ensure the predators are in prison. That's the job. That's the collar. The light with the dark, the weight on our shoulders and when we're successful, people forget we exist, good policing is invisible, I'm fine with that, that's the system and it works . . . most of the time. When it doesn't, things are upturned and this is what happens. This is outside the system . . . and . . . permission to speak freely? Commander, this whole disciplinary hearing is a farce. My record is clean. I've been an outstanding copper since I joined and it is their word against mine. The individual Uhuru Moses was inciting violence and Bruce Okafor was his student, as was his mother. Bruce and I crossed paths a few times. I saw him on the night in question as I had many nights before. The first time we met, I sent him home. Perhaps I was a little . . . heavy handed, but nothing to warrant a complaint and no more than was necessary to get the job done. He was angry, Commander, he roamed the streets taking the law into his own hands. His mother was mugged a month before and he'd started hunting the culprit but four weeks ago he became obsessive, dark, we met that Friday, third time that week.

Bruce   Go solve a proper crime, don't get in my way.

Smithy   If I see you again tonight, I'll bring you in for your own safety.

Bruce   He's still out there prowling, animal in shadows, waiting for prey. If that was your mum, what would you do? Chill at home? Watching *CSI*? Ain't doing that.

Smithy   I understand your anger.

Bruce   So let me protect mine and you protect yours.

Smithy   That's our job.

Bruce   What? To protect me?

Smithy   Yes!

Bruce   So why you on me then? Do I look like a criminal?

Smithy   I have a son your age, I know how you feel . . . what you're going through.

Bruce   Get off me.

Smithy   I'm sorry. You okay?

Bruce   I need protection from you.

Smithy   You have to go home now.

Bruce   Who did it, if you don't find him, I will.

Smithy   Go.

Bruce   And after that I came home, Tanya.

Tanya   It didn't hurt?

Bruce   Naa . . . if it did, I was too angry to notice. I walked home feeling lucky he didn't find the screwdriver in my pocket! (*Laughs.*) I can't bring myself to take a knife. Came home thinking this whole area has changed. Remember playing football all day Sunday, ice lollies, kicking it against the wall, corner of Beston Street?

Tanya   Yeah, that was nice.

Bruce   The whole place was nice, the only thing lurking in the shadows was dying flowers, bleached grass and litter. All that's changed, no more strolling home at night from Ahmed's, eyes dry from too much PlayStation, and you, no more skipping casually from choir, taking ages.

Tanya   Whatever.

Bruce   It's not safe. Remember Mum the day after the mugging, when the pastor came round? Shaking in the living room?

Ama   Hello, Pastor. Thanks for coming to visit me at home. I'm sorry, I don't think I'll come on Sunday . . . I won't have the strength. I appreciate your time. I talked with the victim support unit. They've been caring, really attentive, they've listened so much . . . I was surprised, given what you hear of the police these days. They are great, but I needed to talk to someone I know. I can't talk to the kids, can't have them worried, so thanks for coming. It was dark, Pastor, it always is in stories like this. I had the shopping, I was walking to the car. He came from the shadows, a blur of fists and venom,

spitting insults. Swear words. Threats. His voice wasn't
raised. Quiet, forceful, like small sharp knives, many of
them. I actually heard him running before I saw him,
thought it was a jogger, that I'd breathe in his sweat as he
flashed by but he grabbed me, slammed my head against the
wall, twice. Threw me to the ground, put one foot on my
back so I couldn't turn. Crushing me, pushing air from my
lungs. Face down on the ground. I remember . . . chewing
gums, Pastor, flattened into the pavement, black with mud
and soot. Hundreds of them. So many . . . mouths to feed, so
many people walk this way, could have happened to any of
them, but it happened to me. He bent over, mouth inches
from my ears, making quiet demands after the insults. I said,
'You don't have to do this, I'll give you what you want, let an
old woman stand up', but he punched the side of my face,
twice. He emptied my bag on my head. Took my purse, cash,
phone, bank cards. I gave my PIN number . . . he had my
driving licence, said he'd come visit if I lied. Told me not to
get up, not to dare and he vanished. I stayed like that for
thirty minutes. Shivering on the concrete. Didn't know when
it started raining, but I was drenched when I stood. I tried
singing 'Amazing Grace' but couldn't remember the words. I
staggered around, looking for help, swaying in the night,
falling, standing again, trying to sing myself better. Someone
found a policeman and his strong arms held me up. Can't
remember his name but I'll recognise him if we meet. I'll
thank him. A good man, spoke calmly, held me until a
female police officer came. I haven't slept, Pastor. I try, but
jolt back, wake up and see the mugger at the foot of my bed,
threatening to come in, to find me again. Victim support say
that I will feel this way, that it is natural, normal. But it
shouldn't be, Pastor. Why couldn't I remember the words?
Where was grace? Where was God? My hands are shaking
. . . Pastor . . . I can't stop shaking.

Tanya   You were eavesdropping, crying by the door.

Bruce   No I wasn't.

Tanya   Yes you were. Don't be ashamed, I cried too. Remember she tried to go outside the next day and ran back in, leaning against the wall, proper shook?

Bruce   Yeah.

Tanya   She is better now.

Bruce   Still hasn't talked to us about it.

Tanya   Maybe she doesn't need to, she's been going out.

Bruce   She's putting on a brave face, Tanya, but there's been two more muggings since, violent ones, she must be a little scared . . . and I'm not playing anymore. No more pretend.

Tanya   No?

Bruce   Naa, the mugger's out there and I'm not having him walk free.

Tanya   When do we start?

Bruce   You can't come, Tan. Not anymore.

Tanya   We planned for ages!

Bruce   What? BlackMan and Ribbon? Wiping crime off the streets? You serious?

Tanya   It's a hair clip not a ribbon. And we can be Black Panther, T'Challa and Shuri instead.

Bruce   Naaa! I swear they are Wakandan. We're Nigerian. We can't betray our country like that?

Tanya   Doesn't matter. Wakanda's not real.

Bruce   Neither's Batman.

Tanya   It was your idea in the first place.

Bruce   We were playing.

Tanya   All the heroes have partners.

Bruce   But this is real, and I'm not them. Can't be out there and watching you as well.

Tanya   No mask, then? No cape?

Bruce (*laughs*)   Just my hoodie.

Tanya   Tool belt?

Bruce   Just the torch light, screwdriver. The others will take ages to make.

Tanya   What about the Taser? We finished that one.

Bruce   Give it to Mum.

Tanya   She'll ask where we got it from.

Bruce   Don't tell her we made it off a YouTube video! She'll never let us online again! Just . . . tell her I got it off a friend, for her safety.

Tanya   She won't take it. She doesn't believe in violence.

Bruce   It's self-defence, not violence.

Tanya   Yeah . . . but you know Mum . . . tried talking to her about the self-defence class as well, told her martial arts is about discipline, showed her clips online, Bruce Lee talking about focusing the mind, spirituality and stuff but she said

Ama   Naa . . . It's not for me. All that high kicks and 'Hia! Hia! Hia!' Eh eh . . . No. Thank you, but God will take care of me. Don't roll your eyes, Tanya. When we had no money, God provided . . . church paid our rent.

Tanya   Okay, Mum . . . just . . . please take the leaflet and read it? This one is just round the corner, the teacher was born round here? You might meet some other folks? Get a boyfriend?

Ama   Tanya!

Tanya   Just saying, Mum! Just saying.

Ama   I don't need a man for anything.

Tanya   Protection?

Ama   God and my wrapper is all I need in this world.

Tanya   Your wrapper?

Ama   It keeps me warm and it's beautiful. I used to wrap you and Bruce in something like this when you were babies. You should start wearing some you know? How about a scarf? I can cut a strip off?

Tanya   Naa, Mum, doesn't match my uniform. But it'll make a nice fancy-dress African superhero costume.

Ama   My clothes are not costumes.

Tanya   Didn't mean it like that.

Ama   Anyway, come down soon. Dinner is almost ready. Where's your brother?

Tanya   Er . . . he's gone out?

Ama   Where?

Tanya   PlayStation. Ahmed's.

Beat.

Ama   I know when you are lying. Is he looking again?

Tanya   I . . . he's just trying to help

Ama   Call that foolish boy, tell him to be here in ten minutes or else! A ah! That's the job of the police, he is not a trained detective, running around like a lunatic, he need to stay home and / finish his homework

She walks off mumbling to herself.

Bruce   CUT, CUT, CUT! That was ages ago, thanks for defending me to Mum / but you've

Tanya   Lying for you.

Bruce   Lying for me . . . but you've gone off point, Tanya. Smithy did it. Is that what you are saying?

Act Two

Bruce Tanya? . . . Did Smithy do it?

Tanya Sort of.

Bruce That's all I need. Laters.

Tanya Wait! B, B! Bruce, come back!

Bruce What?

Tanya You can't go after him.

Bruce Far as I'm concerned, there's still a violent person out there and / needs putting down.

Tanya He's police, Bruce!

Bruce Don't care.

Tanya You can't just / run after him.

Bruce Why not?

Tanya He's police!

Bruce Laters, Tanya.

Tanya Bruce, wait! Mum was there too.

Bruce She had nothing to do with it.

Tanya Have you talked to her?

Bruce She. Had. Nothing. To. Do. With. It.

Tanya Wait! Mr Moses was there too and . . . lemme start from the top?

Bruce What? Again?

Tanya Yeah.

Bruce Why?

Tanya Just . . . trust me.

Bruce Don't have time.

Tanya   I'll be quick then?

Beat.

It's important.

Bruce   Okay.

Tanya   Cool . . . alright. PC Smith, Mum, Mr Moses. Scene, characters . . . ac . . . you can say action if you want . . .

Bruce   Tanya!

Tanya   C'mon, B . . .

Bruce   Action.

Tanya   A simple bus stop on a side street at night, old posters litter the ground like large confetti. On the red plastic bench, someone's written 'fight the power' with a thick black marker, there's a bin spilling leaflets out across the street and the one fluorescent light is blinking.

Uhuru *is excited, animated as he talks.* **Ama** *is bored, unimpressed.* **Smithy** *is calm.*

Uhuru   Money talks. If they don't have to pay law enforcement here, we save them money and, given the austerity measures, that will count towards / a favourable

Ama   And what about the officers who will lose their jobs?

Smithy   Yeah, what about them?

Uhuru   Who are you?

Smithy   A concerned citizen.

Uhuru   This is a private conversation, it doesn't concern you.

Smithy   You're having it in a public space and / as a member of

Ama   Have we met before?

Smithy   No. I don't think so. Now, Mr Moses, your proposal is preposterous. We will not accept / any such

Uhuru   Who do you mean by 'we'.

Ama   No, we've met before. Before today. But you were at the meeting weren't you?

Smithy   We, officers, who police these streets, take our jobs very seriously / we dedicate

Uhuru   Ama, stand back from this lunatic.

Smithy   We execute the law to the letter, with transparency.

Uhuru   How many black men have died in your custody? How many officers have been charged? Where is the transparency?

Smithy   The entire police force cannot be condemned for the actions of a few.

Uhuru   Stop and search policy? You treat my entire community as criminals because of the actions of a few.

Ama   Gentlemen, calm down.

Smithy   That policy is a preventative measure.

Ama   Uhuru, step back from the policeman.

Uhuru   You want to prevent crime? First, stop supporting a system that directly profits from and necessitates crime; politicians who are criminals, companies breaking tax laws.

Smithy   Those are separate issues.

Uhuru   Allow me to link them for you. Every time / a young person is

A figure dressed in black jumps from the shadows, attacks **Ama**. **Uhuru**, *on hearing her scream, swiftly delivers punches and kicks to the figure, and keeps on after the figure falls.*

Uhuru   Stop! That categorically didn't happen. Impossible. It would mean I lost control, Your Honour, allowed anger to own my bones, to rule movements, but I teach control, I focus on focus, so that never happened, I never attacked, I've never attacked. I learnt self-defence. Never the hitman. Never the drug dealer. Never the pimp. Never the cat burglar. Never loitered on streets. Never knew my father. But that never mattered, Mother was stronger than most men I knew, taught me never ever to steal, so the crocodile-skins boots, I bought. Never diamonds, but kruger rings, gold bracelets, duchet chains. I never wanted to start boxing, but the skinheads never stopped coming. Never loved England, England never loved me. Packed a bag and worked in Egypt. Never loved retail, a black man with fists? Worked in security for families, oil-rich kings, the ancients of Africa. They taught me our history. I taught their kids boxing, they paid for me to learn about Tai Chi, Taekwondo and Wing Chun. I never forget the lessons I learnt, how to watch your opponent, to spot them first, to stand guarded, to seek inner strength. Never forgot the friends I left and, after ten years, I came to share the knowledge I'd gathered, the things I'd learnt. I came home. Never loved the gym so called mine a dojo, a place for my community, and they came in droves. Still hanging punch bags, thirsty towels, floor mats, but never frenzy, never the heat. Still the commitment, the clenched fist focus, but never the anger, never the pain. Still the exertion, the sound of straining muscle, but never the swagger, never such pride. I never said no, all I asked was focus, taught a combination of Wing Chun and boxing, as I trained the young ones, they spoke their problems, the police officers, stop and search powers, deaths in custody, constant surveillance, threats to harmony, the new skinheads. I wanted to teach the history of our people, we came from royalty, a race of scholars, this country crushed our kingdoms, stole wealth and treats us like animals, treats us like filth. I never wanted politics, Your Honour, I had one goal: strengthen my community, protect my students, that was it. I welcomed them all, gangs that were enemies: train with your enemy, enemy becomes your friend, a stronger community, a tribe united, a people made whole. I taught inner strength, discipline and focus, lectured on action and consequence. If you are late, fifty press-ups. No kit, fifty press-ups. Thirsty? Fifty press-ups and they never complained. We start at four with

As he talks, the class appears and run through the motions.

a warm-up, skipping drills, the skill of the day, always end on breathing, light sparring or fast pad work.

Uhuru   Ready, Bruce?

Bruce   Yes, Mr Moses.

*They do a few combinations, getting faster, more intense, couple of times, **Uhuru** hits **Bruce** head a few times as **Bruce** is slow. After, the class bows.*

Uhuru   Okay. Hit the showers, see you next week. Bruce, can I talk to you for a minute? What's wrong? Your intentions were right but focus wasn't there, you're all over the place.

Bruce   Nothing, sir.

Beat.

Uhuru   They still haven't found him?

Bruce   No. But I will.

Uhuru   Now, Bruce / you have to

Bruce   I know what you're gonna say, but I can't stay in. There was another one last night? Two broken ribs. That's five now. Imagine if that was my sister.

Uhuru   Be patient / let us help.

Bruce   Tired of that. Police ain't doing nothing, I'm gonna find him. He never attacks during rush hour. Waits till around nine thirty, ten. They've all happened like ten minutes from the station. If I get there around nine and follow the most vulnerable-looking person, I'm bound to catch him eventually.

Uhuru Bruce, let us help. You don't have to do this on your own. Since it started I've been thinking and . . . I'm holding a meeting, a discussion in a few weeks for the locals, civilians, adults only, but I'll make an exception for you. We could use your help.

Bruce A few weeks?!

Uhuru These things take time.

Bruce I'll try and come but, doesn't mean I'll stop.

Uhuru I can't make you stop so . . . just be safe, be clear of your objective.

Bruce See you next week.

Tanya! Tanya! Anything to eat?

Tanya Check the fridge!

Bruce Can't find anything!

Tanya There's chips.

Bruce It's cold!

Tanya It was in the fridge!

Bruce Erghu. Where's Mum? Mum? Mum!

Tanya She left like five minutes ago.

Bruce Out on a Wednesday night?

Tanya Yeah . . . you don't know?

Bruce What?

Tanya She started that martial arts class. The leaflet you gave me?

Bruce The adult class is straight after mine! Why'd she change her mind?

Tanya She wouldn't take the Taser and after the fifth mugging, guess she started thinking. Imagine. Mum doing karate chops! (*Laughs.*)

Bruce   Can't wait to see her moves.

Tanya   It's the same guy, right? That trains you?

Bruce   Uhuru Moses.

Tanya   She's with him now. What's he like? Mum might get a boyfriend?

Bruce   Na . . . too strict. Not Mum's type. He's smiled like once since I met him. He's like the black RobCop of martial arts . . . Afrocop.

Tanya *laughs*.

Bruce   Seriously, like naa . . . in fact, Mum might drop out cause of how hard he is.

Uhuru (*laughing*)   Mrs Okafor, you will kill me with these questions!

Ama (*laughing*)   They are obvious ones.

Uhuru   Okay, okay. No, you won't be able to karate-chop someone into pieces.

Ama   That is unfortunate.

Uhuru   You will not be able to jump over moving vehicles.

Ama   Not even that?

Uhuru   No, Mrs Okafor.

Ama   Miss Okafor.

Uhuru   Miss Okafor.

Ama   So what will you teach me?

Uhuru   We focus above all on focus, discipline and inner strength.

Ama   That won't help me in a fight. I want to bring him down like Mike Tyson.

Uhuru   I don't teach boxing for the older groups.

Ama   I'm not old.

Uhuru   I can see that, I mean . . . after a certain age, our bones require greater care and attention, our bones become for the finer things in life, Miss Okafor.

Ama   Really, Mr Moses. Call me Ama.

Uhuru   Ama. A beautiful name.

Ama   You should hear my phone number.

Uhuru   . . .

Ama   So, what exactly will you teach me?

Uhuru   A combination of Tai Chi and Taekwondo.

Ama   You are sure I'll be able to defend myself?

Uhuru   If after the fourth week, you cannot throw me to the ground, I will give you a full refund.

Ama   Brilliant! When do we start?

Uhuru   Next week if you can make the class, but I do have a question, Ama. Why do you want to learn? What's your motivation?

Beat.

Ama   Good evening, Pastor, thanks for seeing me at such short notice. I'm feeling better. The bruises have faded as you can see. The police support unit were brilliant. They check on me less often now and I no longer feel the need to talk about it. I still relapse . . . sleepless nights, I wake up shivering, hear his voice knifing through me. I just feel angry. The unit say it's normal to feel this way. To feel embarrassed about my helplessness, that I did nothing, just lay whimpering and took it. That's why I'm here, Pastor. There've been more muggings. Our neighbours are twitchy, children nervous. Bruce is taking matters into his own hands. He is prowling around, fighting darkness, it's my duty to show him light. It's affecting his schooling. I need to reassure him, to make Tanya feel safe . . . to feel secure, to overcome what happened. It's not about revenge . . . God will seek that, but 'Heaven helps those who help themselves', remember, Pastor? The sermon you preached? Well, this is how I want to help myself. Money, I can make, a phone came the next day . . . poverty, hunger, I understand the mugger's motives. But violence? To be attacked mercilessly . . . I want to learn to stop that. To defend myself. Pastor, do I have your blessing?

Beat.

Uhuru   Ama? You okay?

Ama   Yes.

Uhuru   My question, why do you want to learn?

Ama   Inner strength . . . It's good exercise . . . but truthfully, Uhuru, above all I want to disarm men as strong and handsome as yourself.

Uhuru (*laughs*)   Consider me disarmed, Mrs Okafor.

Ama   Ama, please.

Uhuru   My apologies, Ama.

Bruce   Naa, doubt they'd get along. But he's a decent teacher.

Tanya   Just imagine Mum running out, dishing out karate chops like cold chips. Drop-kicking everybody!

Bruce *laughs.*

Tanya   Some Nigerian superhero. 'You there, drop that purse before I permanently discombobulate you.'

She runs around with **Ama***'s wrapper tucked in her neckline, fighting invisible foes.*

Bruce (*laughs*)   Seriously, think she can?

Tanya   Wha?

Bruce   Actually defend herself.

Tanya   Course.

Bruce   Cause, you can learn techniques, combination punches, all that . . . but when it's time, can you deliver? Mr Moses says fear is the worst human emotion, it immobilises us. We just stand and take it. Fear. If Mum is out and the mugger comes, will she fight?

Tanya   I dunno know.

Bruce   Gotta make sure somehow.

Tanya   Maybe you and her should like do a session here? After she's done some classes?

Bruce   But it's me though. She's not scared of me.

Tanya   Wear a mask or something.

Bruce   She'll see me putting it on . . . like. No . . . that won't work.

Tanya   I know, MUG HER!

Bruce   What?

Tanya   Just pretend . . . jump out the bushes on her way from work, see if she fights back.

Bruce   You're crazy.

Tanya   Bruce, listen. Just shout and if she waves her fist, then you know she's cool.

Bruce   Nuts, Tanya. No.

Tanya   It'll work.

Bruce   Listen, I gotta go patrol.

Tanya   Think about it, it's the perfect way!

Bruce   I'm going now, Tanya.

Tanya   Wait! Wait! What about dinner?

Bruce   Don't like cold chips.

Tanya   Wait! Wait!

Bruce   What?

Tanya   You forgot your cape.

She throws over his hoodie.

Bruce   Thanks.

And I'm out stalking the urban forest, skimming alleys, surfing streets, flight-footed and winged over banisters, climbing railings, quiet, quick when I need to be, slow when I feel, casual, blending, watching, waiting, feeling the city breathing with me.

Smithy   And I'm out stalking the urban forest, driving down alleys, cruising main streets, a symbol of order, justice, peace, slow when I drive, fast when I need, professional, visible, watching, waiting, feeling the city breathing with me.

Bruce   I'd do anything to keep this peace, this silent sleeping sweeping scene, lamp lights flickering, a couple kissing, the odd car passing like a lost ship, this hour of night you look for strange winds, a weird-shaped shadow, anything that glints. I head north, turn down Duggan Way.

Smithy   I'd do anything to keep this peace, this silent sleeping sweeping scene, traffic lights green, a couple kissing, the odd cyclist passing like a lost bird at sea, this hour of night, you look for strange winds, a weird-shaped shadow, anything that glints. I head south, turn down Lawrence Street.

Bruce   Up past the factory. Left down Benton. Right past Corn Way. Up through the square.

Smithy   Up past the cemetery. Left down Charles. Right past Sun Way. Up through the square.

Bruce   And I see him, a slouching shadow of a figure, leaning in shadows, waiting in the dark.

Smithy   And I see him, a slouching shadow of a figure, leaning in shadows, waiting in the dark.

Bruce   I rest up, catch my breath around the corner, waiting till he moves, taking my time.

Smithy   I park up, in the alley round the corner, waiting till he moves, taking my time.

Bruce   And I'm on him, running, he's fast, but I'm faster, clear-headed, focused, bastard mugged my mum.

Smithy   And I'm on him, running, he's fast, but I'm faster, clear-headed, focused, hand round my baton.

He grabs **Bruce**. *They struggle till* **Smithy** *successfully pins him down, strikes him a couple of times till he is still, but moaning.* **Smithy** *pulls down* **Bruce**'s *mask.*

Smithy   You?! Not again. I told you to stay off the streets. I told him to stay off the streets.

As **Smithy** *addresses the commander,* **Bruce** *limps home.* **Tanya** *tends to his wounds.*

Smithy   No, Commander, I didn't set out to find him, that's a false statement. His bruises were from the pavement, I tackled him hard. It was dark, I restrained the suspect; that's all he was. I un-cuffed him, gave another warning, told him to get lost. I didn't file a report. I thought it was pointless. He's not a bad kid and he didn't press charges . . . What old case? Yes I remember, Yes I brought him in. Domestic abuse. He was wounded in custody? Not on my watch. Three broken ribs? Okay, but not from me. I had nothing to do with that. Gotta be joking. What are you insinuating? Come on, spell it out. Commander, what are you saying? What's this all about?

Bruce   CUT.

Beat.

Tanya   You were really hurt that night, Bruce. You got a fever. And Mum knew.

Bruce   She did?

Tanya   Yeah. She entered your room. You were asleep . . . saw me wiping sweat from your face. Saw plasters, tissues. Blood. Heard her crying in her room, asking God what to do.

Bruce   I . . . didn't know.

Beat.

But again, that was in the past, Tanya. The bus stop. You saying it wasn't PC Smithy? Cause if it is . . . I get that, but Mr Moses . . . if it's him . . . I can't . . . like . . . he's my teacher.

Act Three

Bruce You saying it was Mr Moses?

Tanya No!

Bruce What then?! You're confusing me, Tanya!

Tanya I'm saying both of them were there! Both. Papers say the wounds were 'consistent' . . . means they matched right?

Bruce You read the papers?

Tanya They were everywhere . . . I had to research! Watch when I sell the story. Stacks of cash!

Bruce It's not funny, Tanya. I wish I could remember. My head still hurts . . . still bruised all over.

Tanya You'll get better.

Bruce Tanya . . . I . . . I'll get them back. That's what I'll . . . So Mr Moses as well? Fine.

Tanya Bruce! What you gonna do when you see him?

Bruce Don't know but that's two attackers and it's not safe.

Tanya Three.

Bruce What?

Tanya Three people were there. Mum.

Bruce She had nothing to do with it.

Tanya Bruce.

Bruce Not listening.

Tanya Bruce.

Bruce Tanya.

Tanya Bruce . . .

Beat.

She's been different since it happened. Even worse than before.

Bruce   I . . . I know but / it wasn't her.

Tanya   Just listen okay?

Bruce   There's no point / in telling me.

Tanya   Gonna start from the top. Same thing yeah?

Bruce   No, Tanya.

Tanya   Action. A simple bus stop on a side street at night, supermarket vouchers litter the ground like large confetti. On the red plastic bench, someone's written 'Moms rule ' with a thick black marker, there's a bin spilling tissues out across the street and the one fluorescent light is blinking.

Ama *is flirting with* **Uhuru**, *who speaks arrogantly.* **Smithy** *is nervous.*

Ama   The government will not accept any such proposal.

Smithy   Hmm.

Uhuru   Money talks. If they don't have to pay law enforcement here, we save them money and, given the austerity measures, that will count towards / a package they must

Ama   And what about the officers who will lose their jobs?

Smithy   Yeah, what about them?

Uhuru   Who are you?

Smithy   A concerned citizen.

Uhuru   This is a private conversation, it doesn't concern you.

Smithy   You're having it in a public space and / as a member of

Ama   Have we met before?

Smithy   No. I don't think so. Now, Mr Moses, your proposal is preposterous. We will not accept / any such

Uhuru   Who do you mean by 'we'.

Ama   No, we've met before. Before today. But you were at the meeting weren't you?

Smithy   We, officers, who police these streets, take our jobs very seriously / we dedicate

Uhuru   Ama, stand back from this lunatic.

Smithy   We execute the law to the letter, with transparency.

Uhuru   How many black men have died in your custody? How many officers have been charged? Where is the transparency?

Smithy   The entire police force cannot be condemned for the actions of a few.

Uhuru   Stop and search policy? You treat my entire community as criminals because of the actions of a few.

Ama   Gentlemen, calm down.

Smithy   That policy is a preventative measure.

Ama   Uhuru, step back from the policeman.

Uhuru   You want to prevent crime? First, stop supporting a system that directly profits from and necessitates crime; politicians who are criminals, companies breaking tax laws.

Smithy   Those are separate issues.

Uhuru   Allow me to link them for you. Every time / a young person is

A figure dressed in black jumps from the shadows, attacks **Ama**. **Ama** *falls on the floor as the men watch stunned. The figure towers over her. She reaches into her bag, pulls out the Taser and attacks the figure repeatedly.*

Ama   Stop! Stop! The rumours aren't true, Pastor. I didn't seek vengeance, I'd never risk anything like that. How could I have known? You have to believe me. I'd never sink so low. To do to anyone what was done to me? Pastor, I'm not a danger, to anyone, especially my kids. I'm who God chose to keep them safe, their guardian, that's all I've ever done. After the eighth mugging Bruce became . . . and Tanya . . . Tanya adores her brother, Pastor . . . I took it to appease them. I should have stuck to my principles, refused it. I never thought I'd use it. But, against that wall, frightened, helpless all over again . . . instincts took over. I lost control . . . my hand seemed to move by itself, reached into my bag . . . it was in my hand, a line of blue fire crackled and . . . but I couldn't have . . . It happened so fast. Was it my fault, Pastor? . . . Was it me? . . . Okay . . . I'm fine . . . the last time I saw him? It was in the kitchen, the day it happened. I was ready for class, he was talking with Tanya. I entered the kitchen and they stopped.

Tanya   Hey, Mum.

Ama   Hi, Tanya.

Bruce?

It's like you don't live here anymore.

Are you avoiding me?

Bruce, I'm talking to you.

Bruce   Mum, I know what you're gonna say.

Ama   You have to stop. I'm not blind you know. You are becoming so dark, a clenched fist of a human being. This is eating you . . . there will be nothing left.

Bruce   Will you take the Taser?

Ama   No.

Bruce   Then I can't stop. He's still out there.

Ama   It's not your job.

Bruce   The feds are rubbish, Mum. I'm trying to do something good, yeah? I don't care what you, Mr Moses, Smithy or anyone says! Ain't waiting till he mugs Tanya!

Ama   Who is Smithy?

Tanya   Bruce, I'll be okay.

Bruce   You don't know that, Tan. He's getting us one by one . . . gotten away eight times now and we're just hiding indoors. If another person gets hurt, it's our fault. We're doing nothing!

Ama   I'm taking Uhuru's class.

Bruce   And you'll fight back?

Ama   I pray I won't have to.

Bruce   Hear that, Tan? Hear that? This ain't about prayer. You have to be ready at all times, yeah? Vigilant, Mum. Be vigilant. Take the Taser. Take it.

Ama   No. No . . . Listen, when you step out that door, the whole world is waiting and it crashes and burns for someone everyday. Planes crash, you know? Planes crash. Things drop out of the sky, anything can go wrong anytime. We are always on the verge of chaos and Bruce, running around at night, is chaos too . . . We have to believe in something bigger than us and God brings order to chaos. God watches, is vigilant for us all. He helps those who help themselves, so I am vigilant too . . . that is one thing. Carrying weapons is another.

Tanya   But . . . Mum, God didn't help when the mugger was on you. If you had a Taser . . .

Ama   Not you too . . . Tanya, I thought /

Tanya   I'm just saying.

Ama   God works in mysterious ways.

Bruce   Tell that to the mugger. Tell him God will go mysterious on him, maybe he'll stop.

Ama   Bruce!

Bruce   Just take the Taser, Mum.

Ama   You're going to get hurt!

Bruce   NO, YOU are gonna get hurt!

Take it.

Ama   No!

Bruce   Take the fucking Taser, Mum!

He tries to force it into her hands, pushing **Ama** *over.*

Tanya   Bruce!

Bruce   Sorry. It was an accident, Mum. Man . . . I'm done here, man, I'm gone!

Ama   Come back here! I'm talking to you.

Bruce! Come back here!

Bruce!

Tanya   Mum, you okay?

She helps **Ama** *up.*

Tanya   Just go, I'll talk to him.

Ama   He's not listening! Tanya. Look at the time. I'm running late . . . Uhuru called a meeting this evening, on neighbourhood security. He says it's important, wants Bruce to come but . . . You know what, I'm not going. Bruce come back down / and talk to

Tanya   Mum, go. I'll talk to him.

Ama   We have to sort this /

Tanya   Let him calm down first, yeah?

Ama   I . . . you are right. So much of your father is in you. You are the cornerstone of this family . . . I wish you got to know him, you have his temperament. You are precious and blessed. God watches and nothing will happen to you. Don't be afraid. The police can handle this.

Tanya   They still haven't caught him. Bruce has a point, we should have stopped him already. He's just . . . worried. I'll go chat to him.

She hugs **Ama** *and goes after* **Bruce**.

Tanya   Bruce? Bruce!

Ama *leaves the room, returns, stares, lifts the Taser, tucks it in her bag and leaves.* **Tanya** *walks in after* **Bruce**.

Tanya   Mum's right. This thing is changing you. Maybe . . . you should stop?

Bruce   It was an accident.

Tanya   I know but / still.

Bruce   I need to know she can look after herself. Where's she gone?

Tanya   She said Uhuru called some meeting tonight?

Bruce   Yeah . . . he asked me to come but they're just gonna sit and talk, not actually do anything. Right up Mum's street. Man, she's stubborn.

Tanya   That's where you get it from.

Bruce   Don't start.

Tanya   She's started the class, she's trying.

Bruce   Did you hear what she said? She's not taking it seriously, Tan. Prays she never has to defend herself? What's the point? Wait . . . It's been four weeks since Mum joined, right?

Tanya   Yeah.

Bruce   Maybe we should test her then?

Tanya   What? How?

Bruce   Your idea? Like you said, just scare her. All we're gonna do is jump out the bushes, see if she can handle it. After a whole month she should be decent, at least to push me back, right? Just jump out and see?

Tanya   Naaa . . . it was a bad idea. I got choir tomorrow, three songs to learn . . .

Bruce   Choir over Mum? You wanted to come out with me before, right? This is it.

Tanya   Not sure . . .

Bruce   Tanya, I just pushed Mum over. I did that. Never in a million years would I have . . . Maybe you're both right and it's changing me. I just gotta know she can handle herself. I need to. We can do it together . . . or you just keep a look-out?

Tanya   If we do this, Bruce, you stop, right? No more going out.

Bruce   Okay . . .

Tanya   BRUCE?

Bruce   Alright.

Tanya   Alright, then. Okay.

Bruce   Cool. Just wait for me, yeah, I'll be back after class. We get changed and go?

Tanya   Yeah.

Bruce   Best idea ever, Tan. Laters.

Smithy   So, technically I was off-duty. I'd clocked off, I was going home. Streets were empty, night had settled comfortably into the city. It was quiet, calm before storm and that inkling policeman intuition thing was tingling. Back in the day, we wore long cloaks like a cape but the practice was stopped, health and safety or something, but I remember my coat lifted in the breeze and I felt comforted by the span of it, its weight on my shoulders. I drove round just checking for something, not knowing why or what I'd see. There'd been eight robberies, the neighbourhood was tense, I felt it whenever I walked the beat, a rising tension, an expectation of violence, a fear, and I'd had enough. Then I saw him running, pounding pavement, carrying a backpack, pelting down the streets and I thought not again, not on my watch, nothing is gonna happen to this kid. So, I stopped him.

Why you running?

Bruce   That's my business?

Smithy   I told you, off the streets.

Bruce   Go catch a criminal! Leave me alone.

Smithy   What's in the bag, Bruce?

Bruce   Don't have time for this.

Move out my way.

Let me pass.

Smithy   Against the wall.

Bruce   Leave me alone!

Smithy   Against the wall.

Bruce   Don't touch my bag, man, let me go.

Smithy   Calm down. Stop struggling.

Bruce   Let me go. Get off me. Get OFF ME.

Smithy   I'll have to restrain you.

Calm down.

Bruce   Mr Uhuru warned us about you lot. He's got plans for you. Big ones. Get off.

Smithy   Calm down. Calm down.

Bruce   We're coming for you. Get off, man.

Smithy   Shhh.

Bruce   Can't breathe.

Smithy   Shhh . . . there . . . there. Calm down.

Bruce   You're choking me.

Smithy   A sleeper hold, Commander. He'd wake with a slight headache, nothing else. It was for his own safety. I carried him into the squad car intending to take him home when he regained consciousness, drop him at his front door, keep him off the streets, but what he said stirred me: 'He's got plans for you. Big ones.' We knew of this Uhuru Moses, bodyguard turned civilian leader. I drove to his gym just to check it out. Parked the squad car two streets down, slipped my baton into my pocket just in case, I mean he was a martial arts master. Bruce was still unconscious. I went in and the gym was bustling, adults from the neighbourhood lined every wall, huddled in corners, sat facing the ring, on floor mats chatting, waiting for him, and when he arrived it was like . . . nothing I'd ever seen. Silence filled the room, spotlight in the ring and the things he talked about, all of them listening.

Uhuru   The young ones who attend my class complain of stop and search powers, of police harassment; fear in their hearts. And those powers came when this government started their so-called 'war on drugs'. They have been lying to us for centuries. When you can, on your computers, your mobile devices, research the Anglo-Chinese Wars, known as the Opium Wars. By 1839, the British government had set up factories in India to create an addictive drug. Our government were selling an estimated 40,000 chests of opium along the coast of China. Unregulated, direct drug trafficking. The Chinese emperor, fed up of seeing the destruction to his country, his community, banned the selling

of opium. What did our government do? The British
government started a war. Such was their military might that
the emperor surrendered. They invaded, massacred and
killed so they could sell drugs, unchallenged, to the Chinese
people. Imagine. Bare-faced hypocrisy.

Why do I mention China? Because our police do the same
thing. Their job is to uphold the hypocritical laws of this
land; to enforce the government's will on the people. They
don't care about us. They have made us afraid. Fear has
immobilised us. That's why we're not out hunting the
mugger who has terrorised our community. Eight victims,
three hospitalised. Instead we are indoors, afraid of hunting
the mugger, afraid of defending our streets, afraid of
repercussions from the police who are meant to defend us.

Ama   These are your opinions. The police are just people.

Uhuru   Everything I've said is documented, online. I'm
just joining dots. As for police, it's institutional. Mob
mentality. We go missing in their custody, some of us never
breathe again.

Ama   They're not all like that.

Uhuru   Not one should be like that! NOT ONE! We
shouldn't 'hope' we meet a good one! It's unacceptable.

Ama   There are bad apples in all barrels.

Uhuru   If we don't act we will all turn rotten, suspicious of
ourselves, our neighbourhoods . . . listen, I've trained you
the best I can, with enough skills to disarm most, if not all,
assailants. You are as effective as the average officer and, as
locals, better qualified to police our streets, our
neighbourhoods. I say we don't need their hypocrisy, don't
need their intimidation, don't need them infecting the seeds
of our community. Every time you come training, you
achieve step one of what I am about to propose. It's simple.
It's what they claim to do for us, which now we must do
ourselves. We have to present a united front, so Step 1: Wear

a uniform. Step 2: Protect what you love, who you care about. 3: Let nothing get in your way. Over the coming weeks I will distribute leaflets; aims, objectives, targets, goals, ways to go about achieving this. We may face opposition but, make no mistake, together we are unstoppable. Thanks for coming.

Tanya   I waited for you at home but you never came. Bruce, you weren't there. You couldn't do it, so I did it. All I've gotta do, you said that night, all you're gonna do is jump out the bushes, see if Mum can handle it. After a whole month she should at least push back, right? It was simple. I put on dark clothes, scarf over my face, dressed to blend in with the night and went after Mum, went to the class and watched them talking through the window. I almost fell asleep it was so boring. Kept pinching my legs so they wouldn't go numb.

Smithy   I couldn't believe what I was hearing, Commander. I stood outside, trembling as they filed out, chatting excitedly, thinking how much I sacrificed for this job, these people I walked past, day in day out. They just see the uniform, not me, never the man. I was dazed, I walked to the bus stop. Didn't know where to begin, what to say to him.

Tanya   Finally, it was over and they came out in groups. I follow them, thinking what would Bruce do, tried to walk like you, make my feet fall like dust on the pavement, pressing into shadows, must have looked stoopid! They got to the bus stop.

Smithy   Yes I was confused, but did that cloud my judgement? Never, Commander, even when they arrived and I engaged them in discussion, I talked with a clear mind.

Ama   I heard what you said, Uhuru, but your arguments are flawed. The police protect us.

Uhuru   We've gone over this before.

Ama   Run it by me again?

Tanya   Headlights kept catching me out and I thought Mum had seen me a couple times trailing after her but she was too busy chatting with Mr Moses.

Uhuru   They exist to administer the will of the state. They are designed to safeguard the state. The state, not the people.

Ama   The state is the people.

Uhuru   No, the state holds the people. It is the cage. The pressure cooker. The container. We are the ones who do not fit. We do not cage easily. If the state works against us, we must work against the state.

Smithy *laughs*.

Tanya   I waited, half breathing, half seeing, half hearing, but making Mum out in the bus stop light, the bin spilling parking tickets, leaflets and tissues across the street.

Ama   Do you know what you're proposing? Have you thought it through? How will we fund this?

Uhuru   Sacrifices, small contributions. Each community member gives a percentage of their monthly wage.

Ama   So, basically, tax? We pay enough of that.

Uhuru   But this will directly benefit /

Ama   Uhuru, I think it is unfeasible.

Smithy   Listen to the woman.

Tanya   I was hiding, trying to stop the bushes rustling in the moonlight.

Uhuru   Pardon?

Smithy   Nothing.

Ama   And what about the officers who will lose their jobs?

Smithy   Yeah, what about them?

Uhuru   Who are you?

Smithy   A concerned citizen.

Uhuru   This is a private conversation, it doesn't concern you.

Smithy   You're having it in a public space and / as a member of

Ama   Have we met before?

Smithy   No. I don't think so. Now, Mr Moses, your proposal is preposterous. We will not accept / any such

Uhuru   Who do you mean by 'we'.

Ama   No, we've met before. Before today. But you were at the meeting weren't you?

Smithy   We, officers, who police these streets, take our jobs very seriously / we dedicate

Uhuru   Ama, stand back from this lunatic.

Smithy   We execute the law to the letter, with transparency.

Uhuru   How many black men have died in your custody? How many officers have been charged? Where is the transparency?

Smithy   The entire police force cannot be condemned for the actions of a few.

Uhuru   Stop and search policy? You treat my entire community as criminals because of the actions of a few.

Ama   Gentlemen, calm down.

Smithy   That policy is a preventative measure.

Ama   Uhuru, step back from the policeman.

Uhuru   You want to prevent crime? First, stop supporting a system that directly profits from and necessitates crime; politicians who are criminals, companies breaking tax laws.

Smithy   Those are separate issues.

Uhuru Allow me to link them for you. Every time / a young person is

Tanya *walks into their conversation.*

Tanya And . . . action! I jumped out at Mum and she got proper shook, fell on the ground. I had to concentrate so I wouldn't laugh, had to make it look real and the knife I was holding was shining in the light. Mum kept looking at it and I thought she'd recognise it from the kitchen so I gripped it tighter, flashed it in her face. I didn't notice when the men stopped talking. Mum was reaching into her bag and I lowered the knife just a little, just a touch, to say Mum don't give me your purse! Don't give in that quickly, gotta fight! What's Mr Moses teaching you? And Mr Moses's leg flashed past my head and the second one was coming fast. The other guy pulled out a baton from nowhere and he was coming at me, swinging it above his head and I got scared and ran to Mum but she had a black thing in her hand, the Taser we made, the blue line of electricity fizzling and she was coming as well and . . . it worked. Mum defended herself. They all did.

Smithy *pulls back the scarf revealing a wounded* **Tanya**. **Bruce** *runs on stage.*

Bruce Tan . . .

I'm so sorry . . . Shoulda been there.

Tanya You couldn't.

Bruce Shoulda been me.

Tanya Then you'd be lying here bleeding into your body.

Bruce Better me than you.

Beat.

It was my fault. It was me, wasn't it?

Tanya No.

Bruce   The doctors can't stop it, Tanya, the bleeding . . . they can't make you better.

Tanya   It's not your fault

Bruce   Not Mum too. I can't go after her.

Tanya   You can't go after anyone.

Bruce   Someone's gotta pay!

Tanya   I have . . . I've paid.

Bruce   So sorry, Tan.

Ama *enters the room.* **Bruce** *wipes his face. They stare at each other;* **Ama** *is in tears.* **Bruce** *makes for the door.*

Ama   Where are you going?

Bruce   Water. Would you like some . . . Mum?

Ama   Yes. Thank you.

Bruce *pauses to take off his hoodie. Folds and places it by* **Tanya**. **Ama** *walks to her.*

End.